Facts About the Tarsier

By Lisa Strattin

© 2019 Lisa Strattin

FREE BOOK

FREE FOR ALL SUBSCRIBERS

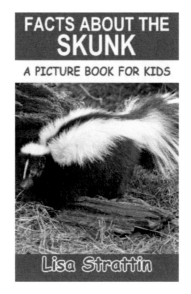

LisaStrattin.com/Subscribe-Here

BOX SET

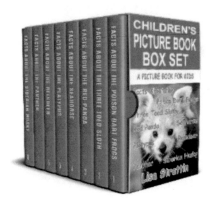

- **FACTS ABOUT THE POISON DART FROGS**
- **FACTS ABOUT THE THREE TOED SLOTH**
- **FACTS ABOUT THE RED PANDA**
- **FACTS ABOUT THE SEAHORSE**
- **FACTS ABOUT THE PLATYPUS**
- **FACTS ABOUT THE REINDEER**
- **FACTS ABOUT THE PANTHER**
- **FACTS ABOUT THE SIBERIAN HUSKY**

LisaStrattin.com/BookBundle

Facts for Kids Picture Books by Lisa Strattin

Little Blue Penguin, Vol 92

Chipmunk, Vol 5

Frilled Lizard, Vol 39

Blue and Gold Macaw, Vol 13

Poison Dart Frogs, Vol 50

Blue Tarantula, Vol 115

African Elephants, Vol 8

Amur Leopard, Vol 89

Sabre Tooth Tiger, Vol 167

Baboon, Vol 174

Sign Up for New Release Emails Here

LisaStrattin.com/subscribe-here

COVER IMAGE

https://www.flickr.com/photos/138134374@N06/24150110030/

ADDITIONAL IMAGES

https://www.flickr.com/photos/hulagway/8622391931/

https://www.flickr.com/photos/rayinmanila/25685444152/

https://www.flickr.com/photos/doryce/301080868/

https://www.flickr.com/photos/goodspeed/179499047/

https://www.flickr.com/photos/goodspeed/179499868/

https://www.flickr.com/photos/peterhellberg/5551104129/

https://www.flickr.com/photos/cyril4494/8645260672/

https://www.flickr.com/photos/137269534@N06/27119834070/

https://www.flickr.com/photos/berniedup/7911590496/

https://www.flickr.com/photos/wurzle/362423300/

Contents

INTRODUCTION

The Tarsier is a small primate that lives in forests of islands in southeast Asia. Modern day shows them restricted to just a few islands in Malaysia, the southern Philippines and Indonesia. They are shy and secretive, so it is hard for researchers to gather much information about them in the wild.

BEHAVIOR

Some Tarsier species are solitary animals while others are very social. The Eastern Tarsiers show the most social interaction of them all, staying in groups of two or three most of the time. The Western Tarsiers stay to themselves, alone in the trees, except when they get together to start a family. They cling to the vertical tree branches, resting during the day. They are vocal animals, calling out to one another from the branches where they sit. Much of the time, researchers can identify the specific sub-species from their calls alone, since the calls they make are so different from each other.

APPEARANCE

The Tarsier has a distinct look – the most notable being their big round eyes! They are small and stocky with a long tail that either has a tuft on the end or sparse hair all over it. They can be grey, brown or an almost greenish brown in color. They have long fingers and toes that help them to hold onto the branches in the tree. They are also able to turn their head 180 degrees in both directions, so they can look all around without having to move their body at all! Their ears are a lot like bat's ears and are very sensitive too.

REPRODUCTION

Most Tarsiers breed all year round and the female has one baby after a 6 month (or so) pregnancy. The babies are born with their eyes open and a full coat of fur. The babies are nursed by the mother for about 2 months. After this time, the young ones are able to eat the same food as the mother.

LIFE SPAN

The Tarsier lives for 12 to 20 years, depending largely on the particular sub-species.

SIZE

The Tarsier only grows to about 6 inches tall and weighs less than 8 ounces! They are very small.

HABITAT

The Western Tarsier lives mostly in lowland forests on the islands of Sumatra, Borneo, Kalimanta and a few other islands nearby. The Eastern Tarsiers only live on Sulawesi and the small surrounding islands. There are also Pygmy Tarsiers that can be found in the mountainous forests.

No matter which sub-species, the Tarsiers live in the trees, so island forests are their homes.

DIET

The Tarsier eats only meat. They are the only primate that we know of that doesn't eat any plants or vegetation at all. They catch flying insects with their hands mid-air. Since they are able to turn their heads around so easily, they are able to look in all directions for food that might be moving around them. They like lizards, frogs and small birds, but most of their diet is made up of insects. Occasionally they will even catch and eat a snake. Sometimes, they catch a bat as it flies by them in the tree.

ENEMIES

The Tarsier is preyed upon by a number of animals in the forests. Birds of Prey, cats, small meat-eating animals and even large snakes have been known to catch the Tarsier for their dinner. Sometimes the Tarsier can escape by jumping from branch to branch since their legs are so strong. But they have to keep watch all the time, since they are so small compared to the other animals in the trees.

SUITABILITY AS PETS

The Tarsier is probably not a good choice for a pet for most people. Although, if you have an exotic pet license and they are not prohibited where you live, it might be an option. But, in many places, it is illegal to have one as a pet.

Since they live in the trees, it would be very hard to set up a proper and safe habitat for them. It's probably a better idea to check at your local zoo to see if they have some that you could see and visit.

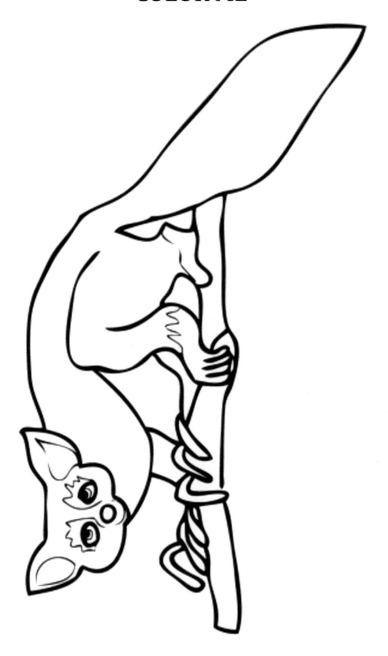

COLOR ME

COLOR ME

COLOR ME

COLOR ME

Please leave me a review here:

LisaStrattin.com/Review-Vol-342

For more Kindle Downloads Visit Lisa Strattin Author Page on Amazon Author Central

amazon.com/author/lisastrattin

To see upcoming titles, visit my website at LisaStrattin.com– most books available on Kindle!

LisaStrattin.com

FREE BOOK

FOR ALL SUBSCRIBERS – SIGN UP NOW

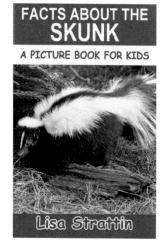

LisaStrattin.com/Subscribe-Here

LisaStrattin.com/Facebook

LisaStrattin.com/Youtube

Made in United States
Troutdale, OR
10/06/2024

23458202R00026